Goals Are Set

By Alek Grigorov

I want to dedicate this book to my great and always inspirational children Stan and Maya.

Contents

Foreword

A Prophetic Dream

To Learn or Not to Learn

When the Student is Ready…

Honor the Deal

The Magical Star that Shines the Way

The 1st Edge

The 2nd Edge

The 3rd Edge

The 4th Edge

The 5th Edge

At the Core

From Theory to Practice

Foreword

If you *search deep within your heart*, there is a chance that you might *find a hidden desire to succeed in life*, to *create the life of your dreams and* be able to *enjoy it*. That's a worthy desire to have. But most people do not know how to *make that desire a reality*. Most of us were not taught in school how to *manifest* our *dreams* – what a life changing experience that would have been if we were only taught how to *design a blueprint of the future* of our dreams and if we were given the secret key to *transforming this blueprint into a reality*.

But let's *leave the past in the past and focus on the present and the potential of a brighter future*. We can lament that we weren't taught how to really properly *transform* our *desires into written goals* or we can *choose to take control in* our *own hands and learn how to set goals and create* our own *unique destiny* the way we really want it to be. It might not seem like an easy choice to make, but life is not about easy. It's about our desire to *learn, evolve and create the life of our dreams*. **So, open your mind to the endless opportunities that will present themselves to you after you expand your mind with the goal setting knowledge that is ripe for the picking**.

A.

A Prophetic Dream

'What is missing from my life? **What is the one thing that if I incorporated into my life today would change everything for me for the better?**' Jim was asking himself these questions and many more while struggling with insomnia, lying in his bed tired and doubtful, trying to figure out something meaningful that would rekindle his hope for the future. Then, after all of these seemingly futile efforts, he finally fell asleep with the questions still unanswered.

That night he had some pretty unusual dreams, but he only remembered parts of one in particular. He was aboard what looked like a deserted ship. There was absolutely no one around him – just dead silence and an impenetrable, dense fog that gave him the chills. He felt his fear and sense of uncontrollable anxiety rise up and manifest in the form of cold sweat running down his back. He couldn't explain it, but he most certainly felt some great danger was approaching and he couldn't help but feel powerless in the face of the looming catastrophe. He was so determined and focused on trying to see through the fog to get a better understanding of what was behind the fog in a desperate effort to fight the avalanche of fear that was coursing through his veins, that his sense of anticipation was heightened to a great extreme.

Then, all of a sudden, he was shocked to see the fast approaching huge, sharp rocks of a nearby mountain that resembled the jaws and mouth of a mystical monster that was going to devour him if he failed to change course soon. And right there and then, something magical happened and a bright white light filled his sight and brought a feeling of sweet relief even if for just what seemed to be a second or two before the dream ended abruptly and Jim found himself lying in his bed puzzled by his weird dream and unable to make sense of it all.

To Learn or Not to Learn

The very next day Jim went to the C. university to attend professor M.'s lecture, which little did he know would change his life forever. Professor M. was a renowned academician who was not only highly regarded as one of the best experts on goal setting and time management, but also as one of the few scholars who were rich, because he would often consult various successful businesses and businessmen for very huge fees in return for his services.

So, when the lecture began professor M. wasted no time and handed out sheets of paper with 2 questions on them and instructed the attending students to answer honestly these questions and then submit their tests without having to fear that they will be graded. Jim found himself staring with blank eyes at the test. The 2 questions were simple 'Yes' and 'No' type of questions and were the following:

1. Do you have a list of your written goals?

2. Do you have a list of your written goals and a written plan for reaching your goals?

For some odd reason Jim hesitated to provide truthful answers. He felt ashamed that he actually had no goals whatsoever and ergo no plans to *achieve any goal* either. But he was an honest, decent young man and he felt like he at least owed professor M. an honest answer to these simple, yet at the same time oddly frightening questions. So, he put down 'No' to both questions and handed over his test and with a dose of shame in his body language sat down in his seat as if awaiting a devastating judgement to be passed onto him.

When all of the attending students had finally submitted their tests professor M. thanked everyone for their cooperation and devilishly asked his audience if they wanted to know why he had asked them to fill out the answers to the 2 simple questions. Of course, everyone was eager to learn why they had been asked to answer these questions and professor M. just smiled and began his intended lecture.

'Some years ago a colleague of mine conducted a similar study at another university and the aim of the study was to find out if *people with clear written goals and plans to achieve them would outperform their pears who had not set any goals for their future.* Well, it turned out that some 10 years or so after the conducted study was initiated with a simple test very similar to the one you answered today, the professor in charge of the study tracked down all of his students and found out just how successful they had become. I bet right now *you are curious to find out what the results showed* if you have not heard of the study before. Well, the results might seem a bit staggering to some of you, but here they are:

1. Around 85% of the people had answered they had no written goals and they had achieved nothing out of the ordinary and were living an average life, which is perfectly fine if you want an average life and income for yourself and for your family.

2. Around 12% of the people had answered that they *had written goals* but no concrete plans to achieve them *and those people were making twice as much money as the first group* – not bad if you ask me considering that setting goals is not that difficult if you learn how to do so properly.

3. The third and smallest group of around 3% had answered that *they had written goals and plans to achieve their goals and were actually making 10 times as much money as the other 97% of what used to be their peers.*

So, the question you might want to consider asking yourself is the following: **Is it really worth taking the time and effort to sit down, create goals you really want to achieve in your life, write them down on a piece of paper and then also devise a written plan on how to achieve the goals you believe in?** For some of you the answer might be 'Yes', for some of you the answer might be 'No'. There are no right or wrong answers here, just your own life and what you choose to make of it.'

After uttering these thought provoking words professor M. continued his lecture by shifting the subject to other fascinatingly interesting themes and by the end of the lecture everybody was in awe of the brilliant mind of the professor and the whole audience gave him a 5 minute standing ovation as a sign of respect and appreciation for what they had learned from him.

At the same time Jim's mind was like struck by lightning – he felt as if he had been finally awakened from a very deep slumber and it all made sense to him now. He was *determined to learn how to set goals and plans to achieve them*. If there only were someone with great expertise to teach him, he would *gladly and most willingly put in the efforts to learn how to properly set goals*.

When the Student is Ready…

Jim made up his mind to somehow convince professor M. to teach him how to set goals. The only problem was how could he convince this renowned man to take them time and teach him how to set goals? Jim was many things, but he was no fool – he knew that *in order to get something of value he would first need to give something of value as well*. The question was what could he offer the professor for the knowledge he was so desperately seeking? Jim obviously had no money to spare – he just had lots of time on his hands and *a burning desire to learn how to set goals*.

'Damn it, I'll figure it out once I ask him' thought Jim and wasted no more time and went straight to the professor, who was being swarmed by many students, each and every one of whom wanted to complement the renowned academician for his great speech. Jim decided on the spot to use creativity to get the professor's attention.

'Professor M., I am sorry to trouble you, but there has been a sudden emergency and you are needed at the main auditorium straight away' said Jim and pointed the professor in the direction of the auditorium in question.

'What is it young man? What's this emergency you are talking about?' asked the professor as he was walking in the direction where Jim was leading him.

'Right this way sir. They didn't say sir, they just said it's urgent' answered somewhat quickly and hesitatingly Jim, who was obviously buying time to come up with something useful quickly before the professor would figure out his silly little trickery.

The professor was just about to ask another question since this whole 'emergency' seemed very fishy when Jim sensed the coming question as if expecting a sudden shot from a gun and said quickly:

'There it is. There it is. There is the auditorium where you are needed' and Jim hurried in front of the professor to open the door for him.

Professor M. entered what was obviously an empty auditorium and very surprised to find no one inside it, but before he would speak Jim vehemently opened his case as if talking in front of a grand jury.

'Professor M. sir, I brought you here because I am desperately in need of your assistance. You see, I have always been a below average student and I come from an honest and hardworking family, but I always thought that by studying hard at school or at the university I would achieve a mediocre life and that is why I kind of rebelled against this whole idea of studying hard and instead slacked at my studies. But I felt lost and I felt like I was missing a key component in my life until your speech today. I can honestly say that your lecture *opened my eyes to the importance of setting goals and creating plans to achieve them and I am determined to do whatever it takes to learn how to set goals.*'

'Well, why didn't you just say so outright instead of lying about this imaginary emergency of yours? I can give you a list of books you can read about goal setting and those will serve you just fine' replied the professor somewhat dismissingly.

'I would be honored to get this list, but I would be willing to do anything if you would spare the time to teach me yourself how to set goals' rather desperately requested the young man.

'Now look here, I am a busy man and I don't have the luxury of taking extra time off of my busy schedule to meet your request' said with annoyance the professor.

'But professor sir, there is surely something you can use me for. I just know that if you give me the chance I will prove to you how *serious I am about learning how to set goals.*'

Professor M. thought about Jim's request once again for a moment and then replied:

'Well, come to think of it, you might prove to be useful to me after all. My assistant broke her leg a few days ago and I do need someone to help me review all of the tests I have collected from the universities I have attended for the last 3 months. If you would be willing to do that for me and accurately record the results from the tests, then I would be willing to teach you how to set goals. Do we have a deal?' asked professor M. as he extended his hand as if waiting for Jim to shake on it.

'We have a deal professor M.' smilingly answered Jim as he shook the professor's hand to seal the deal.

Honor the Deal

A few days after Jim had struck a deal with the professor to help him check and record all of the results from the tests, a huge pile of tests was delivered to Jim's dormitory to Jim's great surprise. It's just that Jim had originally thought that there would be a lot less tests to go over than there actually were, but he had no choice but to honor the deal and hold up his end of the bargain. So, he started checking and recording and at first it seemed like a mountainous task that was mechanical in nature and highly time consuming, but seeing that it would take weeks to finish the task at hand, he decided to actually start analyzing the results out of sheer curiosity.

Once he *changed his mind set and grew curious to study and analyze* the results of the tests Jim *became deeply absorbed in his work* and he was amazed when he found out just how revealing the results of the tests actually were.

'So many people like myself with no goals' Jim thought when looking at the results.

'*I have to do something to change this – I have to start with educating myself first on the topic of goal setting.* I really hope professor M. holds up to his end of the deal' Jim was *getting more and more determined to master goal setting.*

Three months after their initial encounter professor M. and Jim met again to discuss the results of the tests as they had originally agreed upon.

'I see that you have done a fine job with the assignment I gave you. You have indeed delivered on the promise you gave me and you have saved tons of my time by recording accurately the results. Therefore, I believe it would only be fair if I take the time to honor our deal and teach you the major principles of goal setting. Would you agree?' said professor M.

'I would be honored to have you as my teacher and I promise to become an above average student under your tutelage' answered Jim with hope in his eyes and words.

'In that case let's get down right to it' and professor M. opened an ancient looking box and pulled out of it an old, mystical parchment that was folded and was about to say something, because his mouth opened slightly, when he stopped midway as if engrossed in his own thoughts. After a short, but awkward moment of silence he spoke again.

'Now before I reveal to you what this here ancient parchment holds, I first need you to *make a strong, firm commitment*, right here and right *now*. I want you to *commit sincerely and wholeheartedly that you will keep your mind open to everything I am about to share with you* and even if you think for just a second to question the legitimacy of the ageless wisdom I am going to bestow upon you, I want you to *stifle your doubts and keep on listening and absorbing patiently*, for *what you will hear* me explain will only *change your life, if you let it inside your heart and mind.* Many great successful men and women have fruitlessly sought after the knowledge contained within this parchment for years and have even tried to bribe me to unveil the *mystical secrets* about *goal setting* that only a few possess and *take advantage of*. I am only pointing this out so that you can *fully appreciate the wisdom you are about to make your own*, if you *keep an open mind and heart full of desire to learn and grow.*

So, are you ready now to *make the commitment* I ask of you and *follow me on a journey to the depths of the mystical goal setting knowledge* that has been passed onto us by generations of people smarter than you and me?'

The Magical Star that Shines the Way

After Jim *pledged his commitment to keep an open mind and to absorb the secret knowledge he would receive,* professor M. unrolled the parchment and Jim was surprised to see occult-like symbols drawn on the ancient document. Jim was about to ask what on Earth do these symbols have to do with goal setting, but he remembered to keep his mouth shut for he had just sworn to *keep* his *mind open* and free of doubt.

'I know what you might be thinking – you are probably wondering what this five-edged star inside this circle and the symbols inside it actually have in common with goal setting. I'll tell you. *Goal setting is* nothing short of *magic.* You may *believe this* or not. It's entirely up to you. But if you *listen carefully* perhaps you might start seeing things my way. You see, magic has been around for centuries and some even say for millennia, but that is not the main point here. What is more important is that *intelligent men and women from all areas have recognized the tremendous power goal setting can exert on one's life, if one would be enlightened enough to know and apply the major principles of goal setting.*

But let us start from the very beginning. **What is goal setting?** Is it not *a form of transforming your dreams from your mental world into real, tangible things*? You could say – maybe or maybe not. Is it not *a magical tool that allows you to manifest your deep desires if you practice persistently the major principles* that so many intelligent men and women before you and I came *to know and apply to achieve great success*? Maybe or maybe not. Is it really that weird that *a few symbols can hold ageless wisdom that can be studied* with the proper guidance? Maybe or maybe not. Is it strange that a man of science such as myself can discuss goal setting by comparing it to magic? Maybe or maybe not. But let me ask you this – **how clearly do you know what it is exactly that you want out of life?**'

Dead silence ensued. Jim was not prepared to answer this question. He obviously did not *have a clear idea of what* he *wanted to achieve in* his *lifetime*, and he was slightly embarrassed about it.

'It's perfectly fine young man. *It takes time and effort and a systematic approach to get good at goal setting and if you use your patience well, you will find out many secrets this here star contains.* By the way, **the five-edged star** you see on this parchment **is actually called the Star of GOALS**. Inside the star you can clearly see *6 symbols* – one symbol at the center of each of the 5 edges and one symbol at *the core of the star itself. These symbols* might seem childish or unimportant to you right now, but you will very soon find out just how *valuable they can be* provided that *you learn and apply the wisdom* that has been *carefully encoded into them.*'

The 1ˢᵗ Edge

'*Take a closer look at the Star of GOALS and notice the ancient symbol at the center of the edge that is pointing upwards*. It actually represents **the 1ˢᵗ Major goal setting principle**, which **is** called **'The Great Inception'**. *Forming a Goal is like Devine creation – it takes Time, Efforts, Clear Intent and Precision to Create a Clear, Ideal Vision of what you truly want*. That is why a lot of people feel intimidated when even bringing up the subject of *clearly defining their goals –* they just do not know how to begin this process correctly so they can *get their desires transformed into a very potent seed of the mind and heart we call a Clear Goal*.

That is why *you need to have a better understanding of what 'The Great Inception' principle is all about*. And to put it simply and bluntly *it all starts with* **the Big 'Why'**. We all have millions of desires and dreams that reside in the realm of our Imagination, but it's hard to pick out only *a handful of Desires* that *are really worth bringing to life in our material world*. And *it all starts by asking yourself meaningful questions such as 'Why'*. **Why is this Desire worth the Time, Effort and Perseverance and not the other one? Why should I choose this Desire over the other one and devote myself and part of my Time on Earth and a portion of my Energy to manifest it into the world we live in?** *Your Big Why should become your strong Gravitational Pull –* once you have it, *just hold onto it and make it the Center of your Universe and it will exert a tremendous pull over all of the other ingredients needed to start circling in its orbit*.

Think about *what deep desire of yours would be more meaningful to you. Ask yourself questions to determine what would truly give you a sense of purpose, of satisfaction that your heart so desires. You need to choose the Desires that really inspire your heart and your soul and that will motivate you enough to keep you going when you encounter roadblocks to achieving your desires. You have to sit down and think hard until you are able to describe on paper what you want as clearly as possible*. Of course, at the beginning it might seem hard to *clearly define in your mind and on paper your transformed desires into goals*, but *you can employ the power of your Imagination and create a 5 Year Fantasy, a 10 Year Fantasy and a Fantasy that will get you Emotionally hyped up and that will fuel your Persistence. You need to have enough Reasons to want to achieve what will at first begin to form inside your Mind as a Powerful Desire*.

Imagine your Life as Perfect in every way. Imagine having a Perfect Family Life, a Perfect Social Life, Ideal Health, Great Financial Life. Use Imaginary Scenarios to Gain Clarity. See and Feel your Desires fulfilled – take a glimpse of what the future will bring now by picturing in your Mind that which you want your Destiny to bring to you. Combine Idealization and Future Orientation inside your Mind to Create this wonderful new world that you wish to one day live in. Keep asking yourself questions to determine what is it that you want out of your life, what will truly make you happy and bring you long lasting Satisfaction. **What is it that you love to do or would love to do?** *Harness the Creative Force of your Desires by creating a compelling Vision in your Mind's eye of what you want and Create the Winning Feeling in your Heart by seeing what you dearly Desire attained.*

Begin with the End in Mind, choose 3-5 Core Desired Feelings and **Fuel your Imagery with Emotions** *to Animate the Goals that will have started to form.* **Enhance the Colors of your mental Pictures, make the Images larger and brighter, focus on the pleasant, positive emotions and thus start creating a heartfelt connection to your goals.** *Decide what your Major Definite Purpose will be, decide who you want to be. Search Deeply within your Heart to find your 'Big Why' that is behind what you want and think long and hard about all of the important, meaningful and emotionally charged reasons for wanting to achieve your Desires that you are transforming into ever Clearer Goals. And to aid you in this creative and analytical process you can get a piece of paper and a pen and prove to yourself that you are serious and wholeheartedly committed to achieving your Dreams and you can start systematically listing all the Major Reasons that will propel you to reach your Goals. And while you are at it, you can also start Defining your Goals on the piece of the paper as best as you can.*

Here are some of the questions you can ask yourself, so that you have an easier time defining in your Mind and on paper your Personal Development Goals:

1. What would you enjoy creating in your life?

2. What powerful emotions do you want to feel with the experiences that you want to create?

3. What areas do you want to become great at?

4. What do you want others to know you for?

5. What subjects do you want to learn thoroughly and become an authority on?

6. Which area interests you the most?

7. What would you love to learn?

8. What new skills would you love to acquire and develop to a level of excellence?

9. What books would help you on your journey to becoming a better version of yourself?

10. What do you seek to learn the most?

11. What are the top 3 skills that will change everything for you once you master them?

12. What strengths of yours do you want to take to the next level?

13. What type of person do you want to become?

14. What 1 goal would define your legacy?

Once you search deep within yourself to find and describe the answers to these questions or, at least, to half of these, it is an excellent idea to keep the momentum you have going on and start thinking about all of the Material Goals that will give meaning to your journey on Earth. Here are some of the questions worth thinking about and answering:

1. What material possessions would you like to own?

2. What is your dream house?

3. What luxury items do you see yourself enjoying in the next 5, 10, 20 years?

Next you want to think about your Financial Goals by again asking yourself certain revealing questions such as these:

1. How much money per month would you like to earn?

2. What annual income would you need to have to sustain the lifestyle that you desire?

3. What net worth would you want to have in 5, 10, 20 years?

4. What investments would you need to have to sustain the lifestyle that you desire?

5. If you see yourself owning a business, what business goals would you set to thrive?

6. What would be your dream job?

7. What career growth do you see yourself achieving?

Write your Life Goal and your 10 year, 5 year and 1 year goals down and make them specific and measurable. **Think about what your Life Purpose will be and transform it into a written and inspiring Mission Statement that you can look at every day to be your faithful compass on your journey to reaching the Land of Your Dreams in the world we live in.**

Think about what your Core Values really are and how they influence your Beliefs and align your Goals with your Values and if you feel like you are carrying too many old and useless Beliefs, feel free to unload some of them off your back and replace them with New, Inspiring, Motivating and more useful Beliefs. Pick Challenging Goals that will make you stretch, that will make you want to Grow as a Person and make you Desire to learn more and become a better version of yourself. Impregnate your Goals with Intrinsic, Key Motivation, so that you create the seeds of Future Success.

Know deep in your Heart that there are no Limitations to what you can achieve and believe this as you believe in God and you will have removed a great many obstacles from your exciting journey that lies ahead. As you begin describing your goals on the piece of paper or in your Goals Journal, allow your mind to believe the mental pictures you are creating are real and are a product of your Devine ability to create inspiring ideas that you can easily learn to manifest, and feel your Self-Confidence rise; transform mentally your Self-Ideal by creating the vision of your Higher Self-Image as you really want to become. **Be Grateful for everything that you have, for Gratitude will put things into a needed long-term perspective that will open many doors for you.** *Tackle your limiting beliefs if you feel they are getting in the way of your goal creation process by using liberating truths and* **by being an Abundance thinker who knows that with enough Reasons to Do Well and a Strong Will and Unyielding Commitment,** you can not only *transform Yourself,* but **you can, most definitely, transform your life and embrace a more Compelling Future that will be the product of your New Beliefs, Strong Determination and Constant Action.**

Put your future Benefits into your Present by simply **Visualizing, Picturing, Envisioning, Imagining your Goals Achieved and by focusing on the positive feeling these mental pictures create deep within your heart and body.** *Visualize your Goals Continually and Mind Map them and Describe what is inside your Head on the paper in front of you. If you feel unsure whether a Goal of yours is worth it or not, you can use mental contrasting – you can contrast the positive aspects of your achieving the Goal in your mind's eye versus the Obstacles that you think might arise if you were to take the path that will get you to your Goal. Let the Positive Aspects battle it out with the Obstacles in your mind and if you see the Positive win, then that will increase your Belief and Determination to wholeheartedly pursue your given Goal, so you must write it down. Create your Lists of Long-term, mid-term and short-term Goals and expect with fervent Enthusiasm Great things to happen to you – and they will happen to you, because you will magically make them appear for you and I will reveal to you how.'*

The 2nd Edge

'Now let's focus our attention on the 2nd Edge of the Star of GOALS that is pointing to the right. As you can see, we are going to *cover all of the Edges of the star clockwise starting from the top. Take a closer look at this 2nd Edge and, more importantly, at the ancient symbol inside it.* You are probably wondering what it is all about and if you are wondering then that is an excellent sign – it means *your curiosity and desire to learn are still very strong.* Let's first start with **the name of the major principal that this second primordial symbol actually visually represents** and that **would be 'The Organized Plan'**. *Once you have made a rough draft of the goals that you have chosen to Inspire you to do Great things as we previously discussed, it is now time to polish these goals and make them more Specific and also create reasonable and challenging deadlines for accomplishing them. Write a Time Line next to each goal you have decided to pursue. Simply write number 1 if you think it will take you 1 year to accomplish it, 2, 3 or 5 if, in your rough estimate, it will take you the respective number of years to achieve the given goals. You have to aim at making your goals not only as specific as you possibly can, but these goals have to also be Time bound, Realistic and Achievable.* **You also need to break down your bigger goals, such as your Life Time Goals, the 10 Year Goals, 5 Year Goals and 1 Year goals into smaller goals that will get you to your bigger goals in a progressive fashion.** *You have to break down the big goals into Meaningful next steps in the form of smaller goals, so that your big goals do not feel overwhelmingly big, but actually quite manageable instead.* **That is why you need to create a serious, well-designed plan for achieving your goals, so that you can have an actual blueprint that will make your path to manifesting your dreams easier.** *Planning is a vital discipline, which you can easily learn and once you do, a lot of new doors will open up for you, new opportunities will present themselves to you and you will be able to take advantage of them.*

Prioritizing your Goals is a crucial element of goal setting that you must master for your goals to actually lead you where you want to arrive. *There are many ways you can prioritize your Goals, but I will teach you only the simplest and best ways. In order to make sure you pay attention to the more important goals and tasks rather than to the urgent ones, you can learn to prioritize as easily as ABC. And I do mean ABC, because that is a simple, yet highly effective prioritizing technique. Make a list of your daily Goals and put an 'A' next to all of these daily Goals that are a Must for you and deserve to be at the top of your list. Then write a*

'B' next to all daily goals and tasks that are also important, that you 'Should do', but the consequences of which are not nearly as important as the ones you have marked with 'A'. And finally, put the letter 'C' next to all daily goals and assignments that carry smaller consequences if you accomplish them or not, things that in your opinion should fall in the category of 'Nice to Do'.

Once you mark your list of daily goals with the first 3 letters of the alphabet, you can then **make a new list only with your 'A' goals and work exclusively on those goals in the sequence you think they should be done.** *Should you complete all of the 'A' goals only then should you begin working on your 'B' goals, etc. Easy, right?*

Now there is even a simpler way to organize your goals based on the priorities you assign to them and that is to **take a sticky note and write at the top of it 'Top 3 Daily Goals' and then think, decide and write down only the top 3 most important daily tasks you should work on and the order in which you should work on them. Once you have your prioritized and sequenced list of daily Goals, make sure to keep it somewhere visible** *– you need to be able to see your list of 'A' goals or 'Top 3 Daily Goals' at all times, so that you don't lose focus and so that you can manage your time to the best of your ability. Daily Goal Setting is a Must and you can either* **make your list of 'A' goals or 'Top 3 Daily Goals' first thing each morning or you can even do that in advance in the evening before going to bed** *– that way if you plan your Goals for the next day, you can rely on the magnificent help of your Subconscious to work on some of these goals even as you sleep.*

Another goal setting practice that is worth making into a habit is each night before retiring to bed to **write in your Goals Journal the Top 10 Goals that you want to achieve within the next 12 months.** *That way you will have a clear idea of where exactly you are going, and this will give your Subconscious a long-term perspective on what the benefit is from working hard on achieving your daily goals. The idea behind having a written plan for achieving your goals is to* **keep you focused primarily on high value activities day in and day out,** *so that you focus on the 20% of the activities that yield 80% of the results according to Pareto's principle.*

Always use the following centering question if you feel like you are off track: **'What is the most valuable use of my time right now?'** *Commit to working on your goals every single day. Stop justifying why you can't do something and stop* *making excuses and stop blaming others – forgive them and let go of the negativity that poisons you. Be someone with Internal Locus of control. Remember that you have the power to evolve and materialize your dreams with a proper plan of action, so take responsibility for your actions and take the time to make a solid, organized plan.*

And if for some reason your plan 'A' does not end up getting you what you want, then always have a well-thought-of-in-advance plan 'B' as well that you can rely upon if need be. In fact, you can **take your top 3 bigger goals, such as your Top 3 1 Year, 5 Year or 10 Year goals and think about 10-15 ways in which you can achieve every one of these top goals**. *Just ask yourself: 'How can I achieve this goal?' Then list between 10 and 15 ways you can get the job done, which effectively means that for your major goals you have come up with not only plan 'A' or 'B', but you have gone all the way to plan 'J' or 'O' or, in other words, you have a big arsenal to choose from.*

Define what skills you need to learn and master that will help you achieve your goals and schedule time and devise a plan for achieving these new skills. Challenge your comfort zone by choosing risky, exciting, and relevant goals that will make you stretch and learn and apply new things. Make compatible goals and know your needed resources.

Design the perfect calendar and make sure to block off in advance on your calendar the activities that you will engage in that will help you achieve your mini goals. **Remember that scheduling your goals and activities is a crucial component of goal setting, because if an activity is on your calendar, chances are that you will have an easier time going about performing what you have scheduled.** *Schedule your practices and prepare in advance by laying out the materials in advance of your activity. Set reminders that will be hard to ignore and commit to working diligently and persistently on your goals.*

You can either use the strategy to make 30 Day Small Commitments or if you feel the need to have a partner to help you keep your commitments, then you can appoint a friend of yours or a mentor to be your Commitment referee, someone to watch closely if you are working on your goals or if you are slacking, someone to push you slightly back on track if you digress from the road.

Be realistic in setting your goals and don't expect that everything will work out perfectly on its own. Use 'If-Then' planning to plan beforehand If something happens or arises, Then you will perform a specific activity, so that you are prepared in advance for any situation that might occur. Analyze and identify in advance the constraints that might encounter and devise strategies to deal with them and overcome them. That way you should feel more Confident in your ability to successfully deal with expected or unexpected obstacles when they arise. Chunk down your daily goals to their simplest activities required to reach them and make a checklist you can carry around with you with these vital activities.

Be in charge of your life and be willing to experiment and learn, not only from your own successes, but more importantly be willing to learn from your mistakes. **Make your goals visual by creating Mind Maps and by creating Vision Boards that will contain pictures of your goals and that will motivate you when the going gets tough.** *Expect to succeed when outlining your plan of action and cut down on negative emotions should such arise and be prepared to replace them with positive ones.*

Be solution oriented and keep in mind these 3 keys to Peak Performance – Commitment, Completion and Closure. End your plan with your next wish – that way you don't lose time basking in the glory of a goal achieved. Commit to continuous, never-ending learning in your field by reading every day on the topic of your interest. Knowledge and skill are your keys to Courage and Confidence, and you can amass as many skills and as much knowledge as you plan. **Commit to Excellence and Progressive Self-Development**, *because you have the ability to learn anything to achieve the goal of your choosing. Plan to get around the right people who will help you develop your special talents.*

My advice to you is to make sure to take the time and set financial goals and make elaborate plans for achieving them, so that you can have the means to enjoy your Financial Independence once it becomes yours and you are totally free to direct your life as you please. Once you have your goals ready and written down and you have created detailed plans for achieving them, then you will be ready for the next Major principle that will make all of the difference in the world if you know it, understand it and apply it.'

The 3rd Edge

'The next Major principle we should study from the Star of GOALS is the one represented by the mystical symbol inside the 3rd Edge that is pointing downward to the right. **This Major Goal Setting Principle is called 'The Action Mechanics'.** *With a well-created list of Goals and a smart plan of action the next step towards manifesting your dreams is focusing on the actions you need to take every single day to start moving closer and closer towards achieving your goals.* **By now you know the activities you need to engage in with a single-minded focus on a daily basis, so just muster up the Courage to begin.** *That's all it takes – the first step is always the hardest, but you needn't overanalyze once you have your goals and plans. Just start small –* **that's why you had to break down your tasks to their smallest components, so that your start would be easy** and not intimidating.

Visualize each morning the work that you will have to do during the day to prepare your mind in advance for what the day will bring. Visualize also how you are overcoming the Roadblocks you might stumble upon.

Stick to your plan and write down your daily goals each morning or each evening *and when writing them over and over keep an end game focus. Manage your Fears and Doubts by simply taking action.* **Focus on one thing at a time –** *eliminate multitasking*, because it will steal your powers of concentration and will yield mediocre results. *Focus on the vital 20% of activities that will get you the 80% of the results you are after. You can easily apply the following strategy to maximize your focus and results: decide what task you need to engage in and then take a timer and start working with 100% of your Concentration on the task at hand for 30 minutes. Once you hear the timer signal the end of the 30 minutes then you can take a small 5 minute break and once the mini break is over set the timer again for another 30 min. and get back to working with 100% of your focus on the task you have chosen. After you work hard for three or four 30 minute intervals you can take a longer break of around 15-30 minutes, so that you can give your brain and mind a rest and so you can reset mentally and start over.*

Another easy and effective action strategy is to think of the minimum action you can take, let's say you decide to read for a minimum of 10 pages or you decide to work on a project for a minimum of 15-30 minutes. The idea here is just to overcome the mental barriers you might have and just see that working on your goals can be easy – **all you need to do is sustain your efforts and dedication**

over time and *just like the small drop of water that trickles constantly until one day it fills the vessel it trickles in,* **your consistent, small, daily efforts will yield great results.**

Strive to always be done with whatever it is that you undertake. You can also make your life easier by grouping similar tasks together, so that you deal with them in a more time efficient manner.

Procrastinate the unimportant tasks and focus instead on Value activities. **When switching from one activity to another or from one of your top daily goals to the next, take the time to relax for a minute or two and visualize the next actions you will undertake to warm up to the activity you will engage in.**

You might have heard that there are some proponents of the idea to *start your day by working on the hardest task, and that is most certainly an excellent idea if you can have the discipline to go through with this strategy over and over again.* But if you feel on certain occasions that your motivation is failing you, do not despair – *you can adapt quickly and begin your morning with the easiest task, so you can boost your Confidence and Self-Esteem just enough to get you going and to gain momentum. The name of the game* is not instant, miraculous success – it *is actually Repeated, Incremental Wins that you should be after that will lead to Incremental Changes in yourself and that will facilitate long-lasting, continuous progress. Start with small steps in your comfort zone, then gradually adjust, expand your comfort zone, and get comfortable with Discomfort, learn to tolerate necessary discomfort.*

Conquer challenges with Determination, Purpose and Grit. *Act Boldly and pursue your goals with urgency – think about the legacy you want to leave behind and let the thoughts of your legacy inspire you, motivate you to become a better version of yourself. Persist until you succeed and grow your Self-Discipline to giant proportions.*

Master your time, cut down on your Sleep Hours to 5 or 6 if you have to, so you can get more things done. **Create 30, 60 and 90 minute chunks of time and block out these chunks on the calendar, set reminders and work restlessly, perceiving the reminders as an alarm bell** that can wake up even a dead man for it is shouting: 'It is now or never! Your time is flying by and **now is the only good moment to act!'**

Minimize interruptions, do not allow someone else to dictate what you should really be focusing on for you want to work on your dreams and not on someone else's. Delegate as much as possible, so you can create additional chunks of time you can fully take advantage of by maintaining a high level of focus for as long as you can.

Explore tradeoffs – eliminate temptations, quit on all of the time-wasting, mindless activities that would normally steal your time when procrastination would creep in and replace them with meaningful work, because real satisfaction comes with enough work done well.

Strive to be a High Performer, pursue your goals with distinct drive and urgency, become intensely result-oriented. Cut your estimated time for completing a task in half and then refocus, recommit to your goals, and generate continuous energy and simply show up.

Put something meaningful at stake and be willing to pay the Price for achieving it. *Be mindful of the Law of Diminishing intent that states: the longer you wait, the greater the odds you will never actually go about doing the thing you were planning on doing.* Stop the analysis-paralysis disease **by counting in your mind back from 5 to 1 and then automatically, without any conscious thought or hesitation, just jump directly into doing what you were only considering of doing 5 seconds ago**.

Create as many action triggers as you possibly can like the one I just described – counting from 5 back to 1 and just immediately switching into action mode is just one of the action triggers you can readily use. **You can use your creativity to coin special phrases, such as 'Do It Now', that when uttered aloud or even in your mind will act as action triggers that will move you automatically from a passive state to an active state. Use Powerful Positive Affirmations invigorated by strong Emotions to act** not only **as action triggers** you can squeeze repeatedly as if firing an AK47, a well-designed and infallible machine, but you can also use these highly potent bullets of Self-Talk to eliminate Self-Doubt **and improve your Self-Image**.

Activate your Subconscious mind by listening to classical music or peaceful, nature sounds while meditating, to quickly recharge your brain and nervous system and then get back to working on your goals again with a renewed sense of vigor and heightened state of focus.

Be open to new information and adapt quickly, so you can progress faster. But also don't go out looking for all the information you can get your hands on, because that will slow you down tremendously – instead *strive to have just enough information to make a decision and then go through with it, act on it.* **Implant deep in your mind the following algorithm for action: Decide – Plan – Start – Continue – Finish – Complete**. *Let it sink in and don't overanalyze it, your Subconscious will know what to do with it and it will give you subtle suggestions from time to time if you would just tune to its language and listen to it.*

Learn to believe that the World Plots with You – that way with a slight mind shift you open yourself for seeing everything as an opportunity as opposed to an obstacle and your own belief to finish what you start will grow and it will positively affect your workflow. Use past successes as Confidence builders that will propel you to perform better.

But *if you really want to take your progress to a whole new level*, then **you need to surround yourself with a Star System of Positive Influencers**. *Use sincere praise and connect with High Potential People and form a Mastermind Group, so you can meet 2 or 3 times a week with these Successful people and brainstorm ideas that will make you evolve at a faster pace. Seek out who has already done what you want to do, befriend them, imitate them, use your persuasion powers to make them become your personal mentors, so you can learn and advance in quantum leaps.*

Put the pressure on yourself to do more quality work in as little time as possible, challenge yourself and your ability to get fully mobilized and energized by cutting your estimated time for completing a task in half and then giving your best by doing some exceptional, deep work – it will make you grow even more.

Develop and master Self-Regulation. *Learn to quickly regain inner harmony by meditating often and thus taking out the mental trash that starts to pile up from time to time. Self-Control is a crucial skill you can develop with persistence, so exercise it until it becomes your most reliable inner ally. Harness the power of Negative Emotions too by using their charge, but shifting the direction of their power to motivate you even more to lock on to your chosen target and just work with this new charge of energy until you exhaust this powerful work fuel and become coolheaded again. Thus the ability to transmute the negative feeling into positive work will raise your awareness of your true inner resourcefulness that you can count on to produce wonderful work and get you closer to realizing the dreams you are working so hard to bring into material existence. So,* **Act Now**!'

The 4th Edge

Now the time has come to discuss the next Major goal setting principal that is visually represented by the symbol inside the 4th Edge of the Star of GOALS. As you can see, **the 4th Edge is pointing downward to the left and the primordial symbol inside it** may not mean much to you now, but that is about to change. The Symbol **actually stands for the goal setting principle called 'The Limitless Review'. The principle** itself **consists of 3 key elements: Track, Measure and Review!**

First, you need to keep an accurate account of where your time goes and also keep track of the work you have accomplished. Tracking your time is easy, because there are various useful time-tracking applications that will help you accurately record your time. If you do not record and track your time, you will waste a lot of time that can be used for getting higher results quicker. Try to track your time to the last minute or, in other words, be thorough when tracking your time, so that you have more data to work with later on and so that your analysis of your tracked time yields more revealing conclusions. Tracking your time will serve as a wakeup call for you, because it will show you just how much time you think you do not have, but which you actually squander away with meaningless or low-value activities.

Tracking your completed work is also very important, because it will show you just how much or how little progress you have made towards reaching your goals. **You can have a separate Success Journal to keep recording the tasks, projects, and mini goals you have completed. You can write in this journal at least 3 things you have accomplished during the course of the day.** *This journal will serve an important purpose*, which I will explain in more detail later on. For now, just remember to track both your time and your completed tasks, because we manage that which we monitor – if you want to seriously achieve your goals, you've got to become serious about tracking your time and activities, so that you get an unbiased picture of where you actually stand on your journey towards reaching your goals.*

Next you want to measure your progress by determining how valuable the work you have completed really is. You would need to measure how much time and efforts you've put in completing a certain task or a mini goal. You can do that easily by writing in your success journal next to the achieved target two columns: 1. Time and 2. Efforts. In the 'Time' column you can put the exact amount of time it took you to accomplish the target in hours and minutes and you can get this information easily since you would have been recording your time daily anyway. In the 'Efforts' column you can honestly grade your efforts by choosing a number from 1 to 10 to reflect accurately your involvement in the task. Measure your commitment regularly by asking yourself the question: **How committed was I when I was working on my goal?** *Then use the scale from 1 to 10 to help you answer this question and give you a perspective on your motivation to achieve the certain task you were evaluating.*

And the 3rd and most important key element is the actual Review. You have to review your goals daily – once in the morning to get an idea of what lies ahead for you and once in the evening when analyzing the time you've used up and the tasks you've accomplished and how they relate to your bigger goals. When reviewing the 'Time' and 'Efforts' columns grade yourself for the whole day and your work from 1 to 10 to put a numerical aspect to the review and to help you better evaluate your progress. If, however, you grade your work somewhere on the scale from 1 to 4, then that will clearly translate into a red light that you have to keep your attention on. Analyze why your performance slacked and make necessary adjustments in your plan for the following day, so you don't repeat the same mistakes. Instead, you should strive to outgrow your old mistakes by holding yourself accountable and by making small adjustments here and there.

On the days when you grade yourself from 7 to 10 pay attention to why you performed that well and try to duplicate your results over and over again. Conduct also a quick 3-minute After-Action Review once you complete an important task – that way you will let your positive results sink deeper in. **Review the accomplishments in your Success Journal to boost your Self-Esteem and your Confidence and to rekindle your burning desire to reach your goals, because that way you will use your positive past experiences as a springboard to jump higher onto the next higher goal and then again onto the next higher goal, etc**.

Then you also need to block out on your calendar somewhere between 30 minutes to 1 hour every Sunday for a Weekly Review. You would again need to evaluate your work, but for the whole previous week. Self-Audit your completed tasks and projects and mini goals, grade yourself and how you performed from a scale of 1 to 10 and determine where you could further improve, so that can slightly tweak your plan for the following week in order to become more efficient and to get better results and get closer to your dreams. In a similar fashion you could review *your accomplishments for the past 3 months at the end of each quarter, so that you can make a comparison between the results achieved in every one of the 3 months and draw conclusions as to what you are doing right and you should do more of and what you can do less of or totally eliminate. And once a year take the time to evaluate your whole work for the past 12 months, so that you can revise your plan for the next year and aim to maximize the results from achieving the newly added mini goals. Analyze your performance and determine if you are getting closer to your long-term goals or not. If you feel like you have wondered off the initially chosen path, just stop, take a few minutes to get into a cool and calm state of mind with a few slow and deep, deliberate breaths and ask yourself thought provoking questions that will get you back on the right track to manifesting the destiny you desire to have. '**What additionally do I need to do to reach my long-term goals? What can I improve that will yield the results I want**?' These are just 2 questions you can use to make your review more productive.'*

The 5ᵗʰ Edge

'The time has come to discuss the 5ᵗʰ Edge of the Star of GOALS. The 5th Edge of the Star is pointing to the left and inside it you can clearly see another primordial symbol that when decoded will make a lot more sense than when just being looked at and when trying to figure out what it actually stands for. So, let's start with the decoding then and begin with the name of the 5th Major goal setting principle that is behind the symbol. **The name of the 5ᵗʰ Major goal setting principle is 'The Success Celebration'.**

If you have followed diligently the previous 4 Major goal setting principles, you would inevitably start getting more and more of the results you are after and to make sure you stick with these major principles for the long run, **you need to take the time to celebrate your small victories as well as the major milestones.** *You need to install the following Success Celebration process as an indispensable part of your goal setting journey, so that you can reward yourself for all of the hard work that you will be constantly putting day in and day out. You can get very creative on how to celebrate the small and big accomplishments – you can buy yourself something that will raise your level of happiness or make a small party or simply say something positive to yourself with a lot of vigor, passion, intense emotion, so that hormones of pleasure start racing inside your brain and you feel good about yourself and the work you have accomplished.*

One of the secrets that successful people keep is that they are very good at celebrating their successes and thus reinforcing the behavior that gets them the positive results they achieve. So, you too can take a page out of their book and reflect on the work you put in that yields results and celebrate your success by rewarding you efforts in one form or another. Do not make the mistake of postponing the success celebration – instant celebration works best, because your brain will like the idea of feeling good every time you accomplish something you deliberately planned and worked for.

You can also use the celebration blitz, which actually means that you can choose to celebrate with positive self-talk in the following manner: prepare in advance a few energetic, uplifting phrases and when the appropriate time for celebration comes upon completing certain activities you have performed well, you will need to say these phrases mentally or verbally with Enthusiasm and in a quick succession in front of a mirror.

Remember the Success Journal where you would record your accomplishments? **Highlight with different colors and thus emphasize the special victories you are most proud of, so that you add a visual aspect to your success and so that you can carry the positive feelings from these successes for a long time.** *Review this journal and the accomplishments in it that stand as a testament to your hard work and discipline often to get your motivation going, to feel more Confident that you can take on bigger and bigger challenges and win.*

Celebrate your success with your family or loved ones to enhance the good feelings that will start circulating inside your body. Remember this enhanced good feeling and cherish it. Repeat this success celebration until it becomes a ritual, part and parcel of your goal setting mission. *Do not wait for someone else to reward you or give you a pat on the back. You have to be the one to deliberately create the good feelings you want and need to experience to enhance your drive, your Motivation to pursue your goals no matter what. Create these good feelings by your own design by rewarding yourself for your accomplishments – that way you know deep in your heart you deserve to treat yourself right for all the hard work you put in over and over and over again.'*

At the Core

'Since we have already covered the 5 Major goal setting principles represented by the ancient symbols inside the 5 Edges of the Star of GOALS, there is just one more symbol to decode. It is the symbol that is at the Core of the Star of GOALS, right in the center of the Star. Now why do you think that is? We'll get to that in a moment. But before we do that I would like to point out that by following the 5 Major Goal Setting Principles from 'A' to 'Z' you will put in motion a very powerful and extremely Effective Goal Setting Machine that will start attracting, pulling your goals faster and faster to you. However, in order to fully take advantage of this goal setting machine, you would need to make the wheels of the machine start working on their own, you would need to find a way to make it work on autopilot. And that is why **you need the power of the 6th Major Goal Setting Principle that is visually represented by the ancient symbol that can be seen at the Core of the Star of GOALS. The 6th Major Goal Setting Principle is actually called 'The Exponential Routine'**.

One of the major differences between successful and unsuccessful people is that **successful people rely on good positive habits that constitute their daily routine**, whereas unsuccessful people have a ton of bad habits that hamper their progress. Once you get the goal setting machine going you need to keep it going and that is why you need to think how to automate as many of the processes and activities as you can. But how do you actually do that?

You need to create new habits that will serve you well and break old and useless ones that might be in your way towards reaching your goals. You have to keep up the good Activities that get you results and through the power of repetition turn them into positive new habits.

You have to add simple daily disciplines to your routine and then you have to maintain these simple Positive Disciplines for more than a few weeks and after a while they will have turned automatically into Good Habits you would do best to keep.

Now it's a good idea to study a little bit the anatomy of a habit, so that you get familiarized with its mechanisms and equipped with that knowledge you will have an easier time creating and breaking habits. Each habit consists of 4 interconnected phases: 1. Cue; 2. Craving; 3. Response; 4. Reward. Therefore, if you want to have an easier time building a new habit, you need to start with the *first phase 'The Cue' and make the signal for your new behavior obvious – you need to be fully aware what the cue for your new habit is going to be. Then once you have deliberately chosen an appropriate cue that will trigger a craving inside you, make sure you make the craving emotionally attractive in order to enhance its power that will get you to the next phase quicker. Once the craving becomes powerfully, emotionally attractive to you, it will trigger a response and in order to make the same response get triggered every time the given craving arises, you need to make the response easy for you to perform. If it is easy for you to respond in a certain way when you feel the craving become strong, then chances are you will use this response over and over if the previous phases keep getting triggered as well. And the 4th phase is the reward – your response will trigger a certain reward you are after and if you make this internal reward feel more satisfying then your habit will be easy to install, because each phase will automatically, naturally trigger the next phase until this loop is complete.*

Now that you know how you can consciously create a habit, you also need to know how to break an existing one. The key to breaking a bad habit is to offset either all phases we just discussed or at least 1 or 2 of them. Now how would you practically do that? Here are the tips you need to remember about breaking a habit. If you make the cue invisible, you stop the habit in its tracks. If you make the craving emotionally unattractive, you will transmute the emotional power of the craving and you will no longer feel compelled to proceed with the next phases. You can also delay your cravings by employing your imagination to distract yourself purposefully. Another distraction method that pours cold water over your cravings is to wait for 15 minutes – it works like a charm as well. If you make the response difficult to put into motion, again you put the brakes on the habit and it dies midway. If you make the reward feel unsatisfying, you will have to rethink your habit, because without the satisfaction that comes at the end, the whole previous 3 phases lose their meaning. And there you have it – now you also know how to break a habit, so use this knowledge well to break your bad habits and replace them with new, more positive ones. Just remember to make your new habits easy, so that you stick with them for the long run.

You can also prime your environment to make your future actions easier. For instance, if you want to install the habit of reading a book every day, you can pick a book you would want to read and place it either in the evening or let's say in the morning on your desk where you can see it and where it will be easy for you to reach it and start reading it at the time you have designated for reading.

Another neat little trick to remember is the 2-minute rule – do an activity for only 2 minutes – that way you do not commit to a hard and draining activity that will make you hesitate or procrastinate, but instead will seem as easy as eating a piece of cake.

There is also a very interesting rule of behavior that is worth memorizing: 'What's Immediately Rewarded is repeated; What's Immediately Punished is avoided.' How should you understand and apply this? Well, it simply means you should harness the power of Immediate Reinforcement – to build your new good habits use small rewards. And vice versa – if you want to break a habit you have to increase the inconvenience and make it painful.

And one of the best ways to make sure a new habit sticks is to use a habit tracker – just track and record when you use the new habit and do not allow yourself the luxury to slip into an old, bad habit. Keep a Habits Scorecard and review often the occasions when you actively engaged in the activity that you chose to constitute your new habit. Pair an Action you Want to Do with an Action you Need to Do and that way your new habit will piggyback on the thing you have to do anyway. It's all about making your new habits easier to Do and if you make the new habit more motivating as well, you will build your new habit that much faster.

Another useful technique for building positive new habits is called Habit Stacking. It simply means that after you perform a current and established habit of yours you will then engage immediately in the new habit you want to install and thus you will stack the new habit on top of the old one and take advantage of the power of the old habit.

Turn Planning into a valuable and indispensable new habit, then find ways to automate the Action Triggers that will prompt you to begin working on realizing your plans and, most importantly, turn Will Power into your most reliable habit and you will succeed in whatever your mind tells you to accomplish.'

From Theory to Practice

'Well Jim, now that *you have learned the goal setting secrets encoded in the Star of GOALS*, I have nothing more to teach you at this time and now the ball is in your court. It's up to you now to either *take advantage of this knowledge and actually apply it to transform your life* or you can brush it off as nonsense or common knowledge and choose to live your life like a lot of the not-so-successful people out there. It's really up to you! But either way, I have fulfilled my obligation to you as we had agreed upon. And as much as I would love to see how you will *take advantage of this gift I have given you* or not, I have to stick to my schedule and be off to the next university where I have other obligations to meet.'

'So, is that it professor? Will I ever see you again?' asked Jim with apparent sadness in his voice.

'I wish I could tell you yes, but to be honest, I don't really know where your destiny will take you. But do not despair and if you feel in lack of motivation at times, just *remember the ageless expression*: '**Where there is a Will, there is a Way.**'

'Thank you so much for what you have done for me professor M.' Jim began expressing his Gratitude in a heartfelt manner.

'I will not let you down' Jim made a promise to his mentor.

'Goodbye Jim. I wish you all the best and *may God be with you in all your future endeavors*' said professor M. and walked away from Jim's life.

Ten years later professor M. was visiting yet another university and was giving one of his famous speeches. The crowd in the auditorium was giving this brilliant man a standing ovation after professor M. had finished his speech. Students and professors were gathering in close proximity to the renowned academician wanting to thank him and perhaps start up a conversation with him. Professor M. was kind enough to say a word here and there out of courtesy when his eyes caught a glimpse of a familiar figure in the crowd and he immediately headed in the direction of the figure. As he come closer to the figure, he saw a well-dressed man, whose clothes and other symbols of authority and success commanded instant respect. He looked closely at the face of this man, trying to figure out why he seemed familiar to him when all of a sudden, the man smiled cordially and said:

'Congratulations on an Excellent speech as always professor M.'

'Jim, is that really you? My God, you have changed! How long has it been since I last saw you? 8-9 years?'

'I would say it's been 10 years now' Jim answered.

'Well, judging by your clothes you have certainly progressed beautifully. Tell me, what happened to you after our last encounter? I am curious to find out more about what direction you chose to take your life in.' asked professor M. with apparent interest in his voice and eyes.

'Of course, I would love to tell you all about my success over dinner tonight if you don't have any other plans for the evening that is.'

'I think we can arrange it. But tell me this – did the Star of GOALS help you in any way?' asked professor M.

'It most certainly did. In fact, I owe most of my success to the *goal setting system* you taught me all those years ago. At first, I was a bit skeptical if it would really work, but then I decided to *give it the old college try and it's amazing how quickly and profoundly things* started to *change for the better* for me...'

Professor M. and Jim had a lot of catching up to do, but that's another story.

The End

www.ingramcontent.com/pod-product-compliance
Lightning Source LLC
Chambersburg PA
CBHW080446220526
45465CB00007B/2787